Contents

The Presence of God

Bless all who worship you, almighty God,
from the rising of the sun to its setting:
from your goodness enrich us,
by your love inspire us,
by your Spirit guide us,
by your power protect us,
in your mercy receive us,
now and always.

for Lent 2018

SACRED SPACE

from the website www.sacredspace.ie

Prayer from the Irish Jesuits

LOYOLA PRESS.
A JESUIT MINISTRY

Chicago

LOYOLA PRESS.
A JESUIT MINISTRY

3441 N. Ashland Avenue
Chicago, Illinois 60657
(800) 621-1008
www.loyolapress.com

Cover art credit: Kathryn Seckman Kirsch

ISBN: 978-0-8294-4585-5

17 18 19 20 21 22 Versa 10 9 8 7 6 5 4 3 2 1

How to Use This Booklet

During each week of Lent, begin by reading the "Something to think and pray about each day this week." Then proceed through "The Presence of God," "Freedom," and "Consciousness" steps to prepare yourself to hear the Word of God in your heart. In the next step, "The Word," turn to the Scripture reading for each day of the week. Inspiration points are provided if you need them. Then return to the "Conversation" and "Conclusion" steps. Follow this process every day of Lent.

February 14—February 17

Something to think and pray about each day this week:

Preparing for Lent
The preparation before prayer is important. It allows us to physically carve out space in our day for prayer, and it allows our minds to be mentally ready for prayer. The same idea of preparation that St. Ignatius suggests can be helpful in our preparation for Lent.

- Have we physically set aside a prayer space for our Lenten journey?

- What time of day will we pray during Lent?

- What are the "exercises" or prayer methods we will be using during Lent?

In our preparatory prayer, we pray for specific graces. What is the grace we desire to deepen within us during Lent?

- To deepen our understanding of Jesus' Passion?

- To walk with Jesus through his Passion and Resurrection?

- To work on overcoming a temptation that keeps us from fully entering into life with Christ?

- To foster a new spiritual practice to ignite or inflame our relationship with Jesus?

In this week of Ash Wednesday, I invite us to begin our preparatory prayer. We can turn to Jesus and ask, "What is the grace you desire to deepen within me over these next 40 days?"

—Becky Eldredge on *dotMagis*, the
blog of *IgnatianSpirituality.com*
http://www.ignatianspirituality.com/15261/
preparation-for-lent

The Presence of God

What is present to me is what has a hold on my becoming.

I reflect on the presence of God always there in love, amidst the many things that have a hold on me.

I pause and pray that I may let God
affect my becoming in this precise moment.

Freedom

By God's grace I was born to live in freedom. Free to enjoy the pleasures he created for me. Dear Lord, grant that I may live as you intended, with complete confidence in your loving care.

Consciousness

I exist in a web of relationships: links to nature, people, God.

I trace out these links, giving thanks for the life that flows through them.

Some links are twisted or broken; I may feel regret, anger, disappointment.

I pray for the gift of acceptance and forgiveness.

The Word

God speaks to each of us individually. I listen attentively, to hear what he is saying to me. Read the text a few times, then listen. (Please turn to the Scripture on the following pages. Inspiration points are there should you need them. When you are ready, return here to continue.)

Conversation
I begin to talk with Jesus about the Scripture I have just read. What part of it strikes a chord in me? Perhaps the words of a friend—or some story I have heard recently—will rise to the surface in my consciousness. If so, does the story throw light on what the Scripture passage may be saying to me?

Conclusion
Glory be to the Father, and to the Son, and to the Holy Spirit,
As it was in the beginning, is now and ever shall be,
World without end. Amen.

Wednesday 14th February
Ash Wednesday
Matthew 6:1–6, 16–18

"Beware of practicing your piety before others in order to be seen by them; for then you have no reward from your Father in heaven. So whenever you give alms, do not sound a trumpet before you, as the hypocrites do in the synagogues and in the streets, so that they may be praised by others. Truly I tell you, they have received their reward. But when you give alms, do not let your left hand know what your right hand is doing, so that your alms may be done in secret; and your Father who sees in secret will reward you. And whenever you pray, do not be like the hypocrites; for they love to stand and pray in the synagogues and at the street corners, so that they may be seen by others. Truly I tell you, they have received their reward. But whenever you pray, go into your room and shut the door and pray to your Father who is in secret; and your Father who sees in secret will reward you. // "And whenever you fast, do not look dismal, like the hypocrites, for they disfigure their faces so as to show others that they are fasting. Truly I tell you, they have received their reward. But when you fast, put oil on your head and wash your face, so that your fasting may be seen not by others but by your Father who is in secret; and your Father who sees in secret will reward you."

- We are entering that season of the Christian year when the church invites us to test our inner freedom. We ask such questions as, "Can I do this, or choose not to do it?" This can be hard to do with gossip, gambling, pornography, or complaining. What habits make me hard to live with?

- Lent is about regaining control of our own lives, especially in those areas that damage other people. We don't admire those whose appetites or habits lead them by the nose. At the same time, our purifying is to be accomplished, not out in the public eye to impress others but in that private space where we dwell with God alone.

Thursday 15th February
Luke 9:22–25

Jesus said to his disciples: "The Son of Man must undergo great suffering, and be rejected by the elders, chief priests, and scribes, and be killed, and on the third day be raised." // Then he said to them all, "If any want to become my followers, let them deny themselves and take up their cross daily and follow me. For those who want to save their life will lose it, and those who lose their life for my sake will save it. What does it profit them if they gain the whole world, but lose or forfeit themselves?"

- "Deny yourself and take up your cross daily." Lord, I used to think this meant looking for mortifications. You have taught me that my cross is myself, my ego, the pains in my body, my awkwardness, my mistakes. To follow you is to move beyond ego trips. It means coping with the business of life without trampling on others or making them suffer. There is a world here to be explored this Lent.

- To deny myself means: to reach a point where my self is no longer the most important thing in the world; to be able to take a back seat comfortably; to be happy to listen; to accept without resentment the diminishments that come to me through time or circumstances; and to see your hand, Lord, in both the bright and dark places of my life.

Friday 16th February
Matthew 9:14–15

Then the disciples of John came to him, saying, "Why do we and the Pharisees fast often, but your disciples do not fast?" And Jesus said to them, "The wedding guests cannot mourn as long as the bridegroom is with them, can they? The days will come when the bridegroom is taken away from them, and then they will fast."

- Lord, when I sense how John's disciples viewed you, I feel relieved. John the Baptist was admirable, but you are my model, and people saw you as a man given to joy and celebration. People were high-spirited in your company, as at a wedding feast. The feast would not last forever; you had no illusion and would not encourage illusions. But long faces do not suit your companions.

- On most days, is my focus joy and celebration of God's gifts?

Saturday 17th February
Luke 5:27–32

After this he went out and saw a tax collector named Levi, sitting at the tax booth; and he said to him, "Follow me." And he got up, left everything, and followed him. // Then Levi gave a great banquet for him in his house; and there was a large crowd of tax collectors and others sitting at the table with them. The Pharisees and their scribes were complaining to his disciples, saying, "Why do you eat and drink with tax collectors and sinners?" Jesus answered, "Those who are well have no need of a physician, but those who are sick; I have come to call not the righteous but sinners to repentance."

- Who are the Levis in our world, hated and despised by the public? Not the tax collectors—it is quite respectable now to work for the Internal Revenue Service. The tabloid newspapers have different objects of hate today: addicts, drug dealers, rapists, pedophiles. You would sit with them, Lord. They too need your grace.

- Lord, on whom do I focus as I walk through a day? Those who are most like me? Or those who are already judged and found wanting?

The First Week of Lent
February 18—February 24

Something to think and pray about each day this week:

The Desert—for Jesus and for Us

Desert time is vital to a mature relationship with God. If we are committed men and women of faith, then God is going to bring us to the desert at some point to look deeply at ourselves and see all of us the way God sees us. This means we will have to confront the dark spots of our lives and the things we do our best to hide from God and from the rest of the world.

Jesus was no different. He was "led by the Spirit in the wilderness, where for forty days he was tempted by the devil" (Luke 4:1–2). Jesus faced Satan and "then the devil left him, and suddenly angels came and waited on him" (Matthew 4:11). We face Satan and our own temptations in our desert time, just as Jesus did. And just as Jesus was not alone in his desert battle, we are not alone either.

As we continue on our Lenten journey, let us be led by the Spirit to have the courage to head into the desert as Jesus did. We pray that during these weeks of Lent, God will strengthen us in our weakness the way Jesus was strengthened. As St. Paul reminds us, "My grace is sufficient for you, for power is made perfect in weakness" (2 Corinthians 12:9).

Jesus' time in the desert prepared him to begin his public ministry. When we leave our desert time and confront our demons with God's help, we are stronger. It is in the desert time—our time of prayer, solitude, and aloneness with God—that God readies us for our next steps.

—Becky Eldredge on *dotMagis*,
the blog of *IgnatianSpirituality.com*
http://www.ignatianspirituality.com/20689/
desert-time

The Presence of God
"Be still and know that I am God!" Lord, your words lead us to the calmness and greatness of your presence.

Freedom
"In these days, God taught me as a schoolteacher teaches a pupil" (St. Ignatius). I remind myself that there are things God has to teach me yet, and I ask for the grace to hear them and let them change me.

Consciousness
How am I really feeling? Lighthearted? Heavyhearted? I may be very much at peace, happy to be here. Equally, I may be frustrated, worried, or angry. I acknowledge how I really am. It is the real me whom the Lord loves.

The Word
God speaks to each of us individually. I listen attentively, to hear what he is saying to me. Read the text a few times, then listen. (Please turn to the Scripture on the following pages. Inspiration points are there should you need them. When you are ready, return here to continue.)

Conversation
Do I notice myself reacting as I pray with the word of God? Do I feel challenged, comforted, angry?

Imagining Jesus sitting or standing by me, I speak out my feelings, as one trusted friend to another.

Conclusion
I thank God for these moments we have spent together and for any insights I have been given concerning the text.

Sunday 18th February
First Sunday of Lent

Mark 1:12–15

And the Spirit immediately drove him out into the wilderness. He was in the wilderness forty days, tempted by Satan; and he was with the wild beasts; and the angels waited on him. Now after John was arrested, Jesus came to Galilee, proclaiming the good news of God, and saying, "The time is fulfilled, and the kingdom of God has come near; repent, and believe in the good news."

- What spirit drives me in the things I do? Is my heart a home for the Spirit? Could the Holy Spirit be inviting me to take more quiet space? In the Bible, the "wilderness" is a place of revelation and of intimacy with God. I need to put secondary things aside to meet God. God is found in emptiness as well as in fullness. I can find him in the emptiness of sickness, old age, disappointment, failure, and solitude.

- As Lent begins, I might promise God that I will be faithful to the quiet space and time that Sacred Space offers me. I want the kingdom of God to come near me. I want to believe more deeply in the good news.

Monday 19th February
Matthew 25:31–46

Jesus said, "When the Son of Man comes in his glory, and all the angels with him, then he will sit on the throne of his glory. All the nations will be gathered before him, and he will separate people one from another as a shepherd separates the sheep from the goats, and he will put the sheep at his right hand and the goats at the left. Then the king will say to those at his right hand, 'Come, you that are blessed by my Father, inherit the kingdom prepared for you from the foundation of the world; for I was hungry and you gave me food, I was thirsty and you gave me something to drink, I was a stranger and you welcomed me, I was naked and you gave me clothing, I was sick and you took care of me, I was in prison and you visited me.' Then the righteous will answer him, 'Lord, when was it that we saw you hungry and gave you food, or thirsty and gave you something to drink? And when was it that we saw you a stranger and welcomed you, or naked and gave you clothing? And when was it that we saw you sick or in prison and visited you?' And the king will answer them, 'Truly I tell you, just as you did it to one of the least of these who are members of my family, you did it to me.' Then he will say to those at his left hand, 'You that are accursed, depart from me into the eternal fire prepared for the devil and his angels; for I was hungry and you gave me no food, I was thirsty and you gave me nothing to drink, I was a stranger and you did not welcome me, naked and you did not give me clothing, sick and in prison and you did not visit me.' Then they also will answer, 'Lord, when was it that we saw you hungry or thirsty or a stranger or naked or sick or in prison, and did not take care of you?' Then he will answer them, 'Truly I tell you, just as you did not do it to one of the least of these, you did not do it to me.' And these will go away into eternal punishment, but the righteous into eternal life."

- This message is simple, Lord. You will judge me on my love and service of others. You are there in the poor, the sick, the prisoners, the strangers. May I recognize your face in them.

- Where are the hungry, the naked, the homeless who would call on me if they could reach me? Or have I so organized my life that the needy never impinge on me? Lord, you have made this the sole criterion of judgment. How will I measure up?

Tuesday 20th February
Matthew 6:7–15

Jesus said, "When you are praying, do not heap up empty phrases as the Gentiles do; for they think that they will be heard because of their many words. Do not be like them, for your Father knows what you need before you ask him. // "Pray then in this way:

> Our Father in heaven,
>> hallowed be your name.
>> Your kingdom come.
>> Your will be done,
>>> on earth as it is in heaven.
> Give us this day our daily bread.
> And forgive us our debts,
>> as we also have forgiven our debtors.
> And do not bring us to the time of trial,
>> but rescue us from the evil one.

For if you forgive others their trespasses, your heavenly Father will also forgive you; but if you do not forgive others, neither will your Father forgive your trespasses."

- One teacher's advice on learning to pray is this: Say the Lord's Prayer, and take an hour to say it. There is no word or phrase in it that does not repay you if you mine it for meaning and savor it. For instance: "Our"—not just my father, for I share God with the human race. Is there anyone whom I feel uneasy to claim as a sister or brother?

- Father, as I turn to you in prayer, you already know what I need. I do not change you by asking; I change myself. I love to reflect on Jesus' words:

that I may call God my father and work to make his name known and revered. I shall be forgiven as I forgive others. I beg for nourishment enough for the day and for deliverance from evil.

Wednesday 21st February
Luke 11:29–32

When the crowds were increasing, Jesus began to say, "This generation is an evil generation; it asks for a sign, but no sign will be given to it except the sign of Jonah. For just as Jonah became a sign to the people of Nineveh, so the Son of Man will be to this generation. The queen of the South will rise at the judgment with the people of this generation and condemn them, because she came from the ends of the earth to listen to the wisdom of Solomon, and see, something greater than Solomon is here! The people of Nineveh will rise up at the judgment with this generation and condemn it, because they repented at the proclamation of Jonah, and see, something greater than Jonah is here!"

• Jonah converted the great city of Nineveh by his godliness and his preaching, not by miracles. Holiness is a greater marvel than special effects, but less easily recognized. The spectacular is what draws the crowds. Lord, your hand is more evident in saintliness than in extraordinary signs. Open my eyes to your work in my sisters and brothers.

• So often, I ask God for more information—a new revelation or some reassurance of what has already been communicated. But what do I do with the information I already have? Am I living out what God has revealed to me thus far?

Thursday 22nd February
Matthew 16:13–19

Now when Jesus came into the district of Caesarea Philippi, he asked his disciples, "Who do people say that the Son of Man is?" And they said, "Some say John the Baptist, but others Elijah, and still others Jeremiah or one of the prophets." He said to them, "But who do you say that I am?" Simon Peter answered, "You are the Messiah, the Son of the living God." And Jesus answered him, "Blessed are you, Simon son of Jonah! For flesh and blood has not revealed this to you, but my Father in heaven. And I tell you, you are Peter, and on this rock I will build my church, and the gates of Hades will not prevail against it. I will give you the keys of the kingdom of heaven, and whatever you bind on earth will be bound in heaven, and whatever you loose on earth will be loosed in heaven."

- No Gospel text has been scrutinized more care-
fully than this, because it describes Jesus found-
ing a church and giving primacy to Peter. Let me
imagine myself in that setting, under the cliff face
in Caesarea Philippi, as Jesus asks his momentous
question: "Who do you say that I am?" Suddenly
the dimensions of his mission expand. He is hand-
ing over to us (the *ecclesia*, or people of God) the
task of continuing his mission. We are not, as is
sometimes phrased, "followers of the church." We
are the church, served by bishops and others, but
with our own wisdom.

- Lord, you did not leave us orphans. We are the
people of God, with a leader and the support of
the Holy Spirit. I am not alone.

Friday 23rd February
Matthew 5:20–26

For I tell you, unless your righteousness exceeds that
of the scribes and Pharisees, you will never enter the
kingdom of heaven. "You have heard that it was said
to those of ancient times, 'You shall not murder'; and
'whoever murders shall be liable to judgment.' But
I say to you that if you are angry with a brother or
sister, you will be liable to judgment; and if you insult
a brother or sister, you will be liable to the council;
and if you say, 'You fool,' you will be liable to the

hell of fire. So when you are offering your gift at the altar, if you remember that your brother or sister has something against you, leave your gift there before the altar and go; first be reconciled to your brother or sister, and then come and offer your gift. Come to terms quickly with your accuser while you are on the way to court with him, or your accuser may hand you over to the judge, and the judge to the guard, and you will be thrown into prison. Truly I tell you, you will never get out until you have paid the last penny."

- You are speaking to my heart, Lord. I cannot be reconciled to you unless I am reconciled to my neighbor. Forgiveness requires contrition and atonement. If I have stolen, I cannot ask God's forgiveness unless I have given back what I stole. If I feel a barrier in talking to you, Lord, it may be because I have not tackled the barrier between me and my neighbor.

- Lord, you are pushing my conscience inward. I will be judged not just by what I have done in the external forum but also by the voluntary movements of my heart. God sees the heart and sees how far I go along with feelings of hatred, lust, or pride. In other words, I should be of one piece, responding more to God's gaze than to other people's.

Saturday 24th February
Matthew 5:43–48

Jesus said to the disciples, "You have heard that it was said, 'You shall love your neighbor and hate your enemy.' But I say to you, Love your enemies and pray for those who persecute you, so that you may be children of your Father in heaven; for he makes his sun rise on the evil and on the good, and sends rain on the righteous and on the unrighteous. For if you love those who love you, what reward do you have? Do not even the tax collectors do the same? And if you greet only your brothers and sisters, what more are you doing than others? Do not even the Gentiles do the same? Be perfect, therefore, as your heavenly Father is perfect."

- Lord, you warn us against tribal or racial exclusiveness: that is where we love only our kith and kin and reject outsiders. For you there are no outsiders. Your sun shines and your rain falls on all alike. We are to open our hearts even to those who hate us.

- This is not hopeless idealism but a wise strategy for overcoming the persecutor. Aggression is changed into a strategy for winning through the wisdom of love.

The Second Week of Lent
February 25—March 3

Something to think and pray about each day this week:

Bringing Us Light
When we ask God for light, we are asking to know as God knows: good, bad, up, down, all of it.

A good prayer is to ask the Father to let me know myself the way the Holy Spirit knows me, "for the Spirit searches the depths of everything, even the depths of God" (1 Corinthians 2:10).

God does everything to bring us light. In our turn, each of us must get ready to accept God's illumination. One important way to get ready for God's light is to pray to be unafraid of what we see.

We can ask God to shed light on our routines and habits. Is a good habit growing stronger? Is a certain habit more harmful than I admit? We need our usual ways of doing things. Without routines we'd take all day just to have breakfast. At the same time, almost any habit can either enable our freedom or impede our freedom. We have to watch.

And habits can turn into harmful attachments. We can hold on to things or ideas so tightly that we are no longer really free. So we beg God for light to see when an attachment is leading us to sin. God sees it for what it is; we ask to share that insight.

Finally, when we ask for light, we need to be ready to accept what God gives us.

—Joseph Tetlow, SJ, on *dotMagis*,
the blog of *IgnatianSpirituality.com*
http://www.ignatianspirituality.com/15390/
pray-for-light-with-the-examen

The Presence of God

I remind myself that, as I sit here now,
God is gazing on me with love and holding me in being.
I pause for a moment and think of this.

Freedom

"There are very few people who realize what God would make of them if they abandoned themselves into his hands, and let themselves be formed by his grace" (St. Ignatius). I ask for the grace to trust myself totally to God's love.

Consciousness

Where do I sense hope, encouragement, and growth in my life? By looking back over the past few months, I may be able to see which activities and occasions have produced rich fruit. If I do notice such areas, I will determine to give those areas both time and space in the future.

The Word

Lord Jesus, you became human to communicate with me.
You walked and worked on this earth.
You endured the heat and struggled with the cold.
All your time on this earth was spent in caring for humanity.

You healed the sick, you raised the dead.
Most important of all, you saved me from death.
(Please turn to the Scripture on the following pages.
Inspiration points are there should you need them.
When you are ready, return here to continue.)

Conversation
What is stirring in me as I pray? Am I consoled, troubled, left cold? I imagine Jesus standing or sitting at my side, and I share my feelings with him.

Conclusion
Glory be to the Father, and to the Son, and to the Holy Spirit,
As it was in the beginning, is now and ever shall be,
World without end. Amen.

Sunday 25th February
Second Sunday of Lent

Mark 9:2–10

Six days later, Jesus took with him Peter and James and John, and led them up a high mountain apart, by themselves. And he was transfigured before them, and his clothes became dazzling white, such as no one on earth could bleach them. And there appeared to them Elijah with Moses, who were talking with Jesus. Then Peter said to Jesus, "Rabbi, it is good for us to be here; let us make three dwellings, one for you, one for Moses, and one for Elijah." He did not know what to say, for they were terrified. Then a cloud overshadowed them, and from the cloud there came a voice, "This is my Son, the Beloved; listen to him!" Suddenly when they looked around, they saw no one with them any more, but only Jesus. // As they were coming down the mountain, he ordered them to tell no one about what they had seen, until after the Son of Man had risen from the dead. So they kept the matter to themselves, questioning what this rising from the dead could mean.

- In our journey to God, we have peak moments, when the ground is holy. Like Peter, we want them to last forever. But Jesus brings us down the mountain and prepares us for the hard times ahead, during which we live on the memory of brief transfigurations. Can I recall any of my peak moments?

- There was glory in this experience, but also fear. I want God's presence and revelation, but am I willing to stand in places that are unfamiliar to me?

Monday 26th February
Luke 6:36–38

Jesus said to the disciples, "Be merciful, just as your Father is merciful. Do not judge, and you will not be judged; do not condemn, and you will not be condemned. Forgive, and you will be forgiven; give, and it will be given to you. A good measure, pressed down, shaken together, running over, will be put into your lap; for the measure you give will be the measure you get back."

- Lord, my lap and my hands are open to receive from you; you tell me they will not be able to contain the cascade of blessings from your hand, provided my hands are open to give as well as to receive. You respond in a superabundant way when we generously share what we have. I remember the old Dean in *Babette's Feast*: "The only things which we may take with us from our life on earth are those which we have given away."

- "Do not judge." It can take a lifetime to unlearn this habit, can't it? Holy Spirit, alert me when my mind and heart revert to this damaging response toward others.

Tuesday 27th February
Matthew 23:1–12

Then Jesus said to the crowds and to his disciples, "The scribes and the Pharisees sit on Moses' seat; therefore, do whatever they teach you and follow it; but do not do as they do, for they do not practice what they teach. They tie up heavy burdens, hard to bear, and lay them on the shoulders of others; but they themselves are unwilling to lift a finger to move them. They do all their deeds to be seen by others; for they make their phylacteries broad and their fringes long. They love to have the place of honor at banquets and the best seats in the synagogues, and to be greeted with respect in the marketplaces, and to have people call them rabbi. But you are not to be called rabbi, for you have one teacher, and you are all students. And call no one your father on earth, for you have one Father—the one in heaven. Nor are you to be called instructors, for you have one instructor, the Messiah. The greatest among you will be your servant. All who exalt themselves will be humbled, and all who humble themselves will be exalted."

• Lord, you pick out the manifestations of vanity and self-importance. "You are all students," you say. In the mysterious way that Scripture works, I am growing daily in knowledge of God's ways. You, Lord, are my teacher.

• The Christian identity is servant, disciple, humble follower. Greatness is seen in love, in our willingness to serve others as Jesus did. Many cultures and groups of people honor success, wealth, and self-importance. Remember in prayer a moment when you felt humbled as you served somebody or did something truly relevant for them. Offer this memory to God in thanks.

Wednesday 28th February
Matthew 20:17–28

While Jesus was going up to Jerusalem, he took the twelve disciples aside by themselves, and said to them on the way, "See, we are going up to Jerusalem, and the Son of Man will be handed over to the chief priests and scribes, and they will condemn him to death; then they will hand him over to the Gentiles to be mocked and flogged and crucified; and on the third day he will be raised." // Then the mother of the sons of Zebedee came to him with her sons, and kneeling before him, she asked a favor of him. And he said to her, "What do you want?" She said to him, "Declare that these two sons of mine will sit, one at your right hand and one at your left, in your kingdom." But Jesus answered, "You do not know what you are asking. Are you able to drink the cup that I am about to drink? They said to him, "We are able." He said to them, "You will indeed drink my cup, but to sit at my right hand and at my left, this is not mine to grant, but it is for those for whom it has been prepared by my Father." // When the ten heard it, they were angry with the two brothers. But Jesus called them to him and said, "You know that the rulers of the Gentiles lord it over them, and their great ones are tyrants over them. It will not be so among you; but whoever wishes to be great among you must be your servant, and whoever wishes to be first among you must be your slave; just as the Son of Man came not to be served but to serve, and to give his life a ransom for many."

- Perhaps, when they heard of Jesus' impending death, these two men and their mother were thinking, *Who will succeed Jesus? What is going to happen?* After so much time with Jesus, his disciples still thought more in terms of an earthly kind of kingdom and power. How often do I slip into this way of thinking?

- Jesus does not present a positive picture of "the Gentiles"; he refers to a style of ruling over others that was never meant to be found among God's people, going all the way back to the prophets and kings of Israel. What would a "servant" look like in my time and culture, and how could I behave more like a servant?

Thursday 1st March
Luke 16:19–31

Jesus said to the Pharisees, "There was a rich man who was dressed in purple and fine linen and who feasted sumptuously every day. And at his gate lay a poor man named Lazarus, covered with sores, who longed to satisfy his hunger with what fell from the rich man's table; even the dogs would come and lick his sores. The poor man died and was carried away by the angels to be with Abraham. The rich man also died and was buried. In Hades, where he was being tormented, he looked up and saw Abraham far away with Lazarus by his side. He called out, 'Father Abraham, have mercy on me, and send Lazarus to dip the tip of his finger in water and cool my tongue; for I am in agony in these flames.' But Abraham said, 'Child, remember that during your lifetime you received your good things, and Lazarus in like manner evil things; but now he is comforted here, and you are in agony. Besides all this, between you and us a great chasm has been fixed, so that those who might want to pass from here to you cannot do so, and no one can cross from there to us.' He said, 'Then, father, I beg you to send him to my father's house—for I have five brothers—that he may warn them, so that they will not also come into this place of torment.' Abraham replied, 'They have Moses and the prophets; they should listen to them.' He said, 'No, father Abraham; but if someone goes to them from the dead, they will repent.' He said to him, 'If they do not listen to Moses and the prophets, neither will they be convinced even if someone rises from the dead.'"

• This is a parable of startling contrasts, but its central message is simple: be alert to the needs under your nose. It is not concerned with patterns of good living on the part of Lazarus nor of evildoing on the part of the rich man. But the latter closed his eyes to the needy at his gate.

• Without an eye for those in need around us, our life becomes self-centered and callous. Jesus is asking his listeners to open their eyes to what is right in front of them and to open their ears to the simple command of the Gospel: love your neighbor.

Friday 2nd March
Matthew 21:33–43, 45–46

Jesus said: "Listen to another parable. There was a landowner who planted a vineyard, put a fence around it, dug a wine press in it, and built a watchtower. Then he leased it to tenants and went to another country. When the harvest time had come, he sent his slaves to the tenants to collect his produce. But the tenants seized his slaves and beat one, killed another, and stoned another. Again he sent other slaves, more than the first; and they treated them in the same way. Finally he sent his son to them, saying, 'They will respect my son.' But when the tenants saw the son, they said to themselves, 'This is the heir; come, let us kill him and get his inheritance.' So they seized him, threw him out of the vineyard, and killed him. Now when the owner of the vineyard comes, what will he do to those tenants?" They said to him, "He will put those wretches to a miserable death, and lease the vineyard to other tenants who will give him the produce at the harvest time." // Jesus said to them, "Have you never read in the scriptures:

'The stone that the builders rejected
    has become the cornerstone;
this was the Lord's doing,
    and it is amazing in our eyes'?

Therefore I tell you, the kingdom of God will be taken away from you and given to a people that produces the fruits of the kingdom. When the chief priests and the Pharisees heard his parables, they realized that he was speaking about them. They wanted to arrest him, but they feared the crowds, because they regarded him as a prophet.

- Lord, this parable is about the Jews rejecting Jesus as Messiah. But it is also about me. I am the tenant of your vineyard. For me you have planted and protected a crop, and from me you expect some harvest. The fruit is for you, not for me. I may feel annoyed when you ask, but you are right to expect something of me.

- As I look at my life today, what do I see that God has entrusted to me? What might God expect from me? And what is my response?

Saturday 3rd March
Luke 15:1–3, 11–32

Now all the tax collectors and sinners were coming near to listen to him. And the Pharisees and the scribes were grumbling and saying, "This fellow welcomes sinners and eats with them." So he told them this parable: // "There was a man who had two sons. The younger of them said to his father, 'Father, give me the share of the property that will belong to me.' So he divided his property between them. A few days later the younger son gathered all he had and travelled to a distant country, and there he squandered his property in dissolute living. When he had spent everything, a severe famine took place throughout that country, and he began to be in need. So he went and hired himself out to one of the citizens of that country, who sent him to his fields to feed the pigs. He would gladly have filled himself with the pods that the pigs were eating; and no one gave him anything. But when he came to himself he said, 'How many of my father's hired hands have bread enough and to spare, but here I am dying of hunger! I will get up and go to my father, and I will say to him, "Father, I have sinned against heaven and before you; I am no longer worthy to be called your son; treat me like one of your hired hands."' So he set off and went to his father. But while he was still far off, his father saw him and was filled with compassion; he ran and put his arms around him and kissed him. Then the son said to him, 'Father, I have sinned against heaven and before you; I am no longer worthy to be called your son.' But the father said to his slaves, 'Quickly, bring out a robe—the best one—and put it on him; put a ring on his finger and sandals on his feet. And get the fatted calf and kill it, and let us eat and celebrate; for this son of mine was dead and is alive again; he was lost and is found!' And they began to celebrate. // "Now his elder son was in the field; and when he came and approached the house, he heard music and dancing. He called one of the slaves and asked what was going on. He replied, 'Your brother has come, and your father has killed the fatted calf, because he has got him back safe and sound.' Then he became angry and refused to go in. His father came out and began to plead with him. But he answered his father, 'Listen! For all these years I have been working like a slave for you, and I have never disobeyed your command; yet you have never given me even a young goat so that I might celebrate with my friends. But when this son of yours came back, who has devoured your property with prostitutes, you killed the fatted calf for him!' Then the father said to him, 'Son, you are always with me, and all that is mine is yours. But we had to celebrate and rejoice, because this brother of yours was dead and has come to life; he was lost and has been found.'"

- The parable of the prodigal son gives me a picture of the steadfast love of God. There, Lord, you show how your heavenly father would appear in human form. When he welcomes back his lost son with tears of delight, kills the fatted calf, brings out the best robe, and throws a great party, it is not to please other people but to give expression to his own overwhelming pleasure that his child has come home.

- Can I believe that God delights in me as much as he delights in the lost son of this parable?

The Third Week of Lent
March 4—March 10

Something to think and pray about each day this week:

Our Inheritance

[In the parable of the forgiving father, the younger son returned home and] was welcomed, forgiven, and restored to full sonship. . . . The son had been lost and found. Now he knew what it meant to be his father's son. He was home! The father was overjoyed: "My son has come to life; let the celebration begin!"

No sooner had the music and dancing begun than the other, older son stormed in and confronted their father. However disappointed the father may have been by the older son's resentment and ill will, he had the wisdom not to take sides. He may have sensed that the older son was suffering an alienation of his own. The older son's attitudes had distanced him from his brother to such an extent that he referred to him not as "my brother" but as "this son of yours." His self-righteous attitudes had prevented him from entering into a loving relationship, not only with his brother but also with his father. The elder son, too, was lost; he was lost in a foreign land of his own making.

The father responded as he had with his younger son. He was compassionate. He did not ridicule his son but rebuked him gently. "You are always with me, and all that is mine is yours." All the father was able to do was invite the son to confront his negativity, accept his own position, and enter into the joy of his brother's return.

As sons and daughters of our Father, we are invited to claim the reality of our inheritance as sons and daughters of a loving and merciful God. The banquet is prepared. Will you enter into the joy of your Father?

—Jacqueline Syrup Bergan and Sister Marie Schwan, CSJ,
Forgiveness: A Guide for Prayer

The Presence of God
I pause for a moment
and reflect on God's life-giving presence
in every part of my body,
in everything around me,
in the whole of my life.

Freedom
Many countries are at this moment suffering the agonies of war. I bow my head in thanksgiving for my freedom. I pray for all prisoners and captives.

Consciousness
Knowing that God loves me unconditionally, I look honestly over the past day, its events, and my feelings. Do I have something to be grateful for? Then I give thanks. Is there something I am sorry for? Then I ask forgiveness.

The Word
Now I turn to the Scripture set out for me this day. I read slowly over the words and see if any sentence or sentiment appeals to me. (Please turn to the Scripture on the following pages. Inspiration points are there should you need them. When you are ready, return here to continue.)

Conversation
I know with certainty that there were times when you carried me, Lord. There were times when it was through your strength that I got through the dark times in my life.

Conclusion
Glory be to the Father, and to the Son, and to the Holy Spirit,
As it was in the beginning, is now and ever shall be,
World without end. Amen.

Sunday 4th March
Third Sunday of Lent
John 2:13–25

The Passover of the Jews was near, and Jesus went up to Jerusalem. In the temple he found people selling cattle, sheep, and doves, and the money changers seated at their tables. Making a whip of cords, he drove all of them out of the temple, both the sheep and the cattle. He also poured out the coins of the money changers and overturned their tables. He told those who were selling the doves, "Take these things out of here! Stop making my Father's house a marketplace!" His disciples remembered that it was written, "Zeal for your house will consume me." The Jews then said to him, "What sign can you show us for doing this?" Jesus answered them, "Destroy this temple, and in three days I will raise it up." The Jews then said, "This temple has been under construction for forty-six years, and will you raise it up in three days?" But he was speaking of the temple of his body. After he was raised from the dead, his disciples remembered that he had said this; and they believed the scripture and the word that Jesus had spoken. // When he was in Jerusalem during the Passover festival, many believed in his name because they saw the signs that he was doing. But Jesus on his part would not entrust himself to them, because he knew all people and needed no one to testify about anyone; for he himself knew what was in everyone.

- I imagine myself visiting the temple when Jesus enters. I am accustomed to the money changers and to the hucksters who convenience worshippers by selling cattle, sheep, and doves for the ritual sacrifices. The fury of Jesus startles and upsets me, makes me think. Surely these guys are making honest money?

- But this is the house of God. When money creeps in, it tends to take over. Are any of the Christian sacraments untouched by commercialism? Christening parties, first communion money, confirmation dances, and wedding feasts—they are meant to be the touch of God at key moments in our lives; but can God get a hearing amid the clatter of coins?

Monday 5th March
Luke 4:24–30

And he said, "Truly I tell you, no prophet is accepted in the prophet's hometown. But the truth is, there were many widows in Israel in the time of Elijah, when the heaven was shut up three years and six months, and there was a severe famine over all the land; yet Elijah was sent to none of them except to a widow at Zarephath in Sidon. There were also many lepers in Israel in the time of the prophet Elisha, and none of them was cleansed except Naaman the Syrian." When they heard this, all in the synagogue were filled with rage. They got up, drove him out of the town, and led him to the brow of the hill on which their town was built, so that they might hurl him off the cliff. But he passed through the midst of them and went on his way.

- This is about the expectation of miracles and cures. The self-important Naaman felt he had been slighted: he met only a messenger, not the prophet himself; and the cure depended on Naaman washing himself in the river instead of receiving hands-on treatment by Elisha.

- I am the same, Lord. Even in my neediness my ego pushes through. I want to be not just a victim but a celebrity victim. I want not just a cure but to be the center of attention. Help me center on you, not myself.

Tuesday 6th March
Matthew 18:21–35

Then Peter came and said to him, "Lord, if another member of the church sins against me, how often should I forgive? As many as seven times?" Jesus said to him, "Not seven times, but, I tell you, seventy-seven times." // "For this reason the kingdom of heaven may be compared to a king who wished to settle accounts with his slaves. When he began the reckoning, one who owed him ten thousand talents was brought to him; and, as he could not pay, his lord ordered him to be sold, together with his wife and children and all his possessions, and payment to be made. So the slave fell on his knees before him, saying, 'Have patience with me, and I will pay you everything.' And out of pity for him, the lord of that slave released him and forgave him the debt. But that same slave, as he went out, came upon one of his fellow slaves who owed him a hundred denarii; and seizing him by the throat, he said, 'Pay what you owe.' Then his fellow slave fell down and pleaded with him, 'Have patience with me, and I will pay you.' But he refused; then he went and threw him into prison until he would pay the debt. When his fellow slaves saw what had happened, they were greatly distressed, and they went and reported to their lord all that had taken place. Then his lord summoned him and said to him, 'You wicked slave! I forgave you all that debt because you pleaded with me. Should you not have had mercy on your fellow slave, as I had mercy on you?' And in anger his lord handed him over to be tortured until he would pay his entire debt. So my heavenly Father will also do to every one of you, if you do not forgive your brother or sister from your heart."

- There is no limit to the number of times we are called to forgive. This is one of the most demanding aspects of Christ's teaching. Yet forgiveness is a grace for the one offering it as well as for the one receiving it.

- When is it most difficult for me to be merciful? Do I feel that a person must somehow deserve my mercy?

Wednesday 7th March
Matthew 5:17–19

"Do not think that I have come to abolish the law or the prophets; I have come not to abolish but to fulfill. For truly I tell you, until heaven and earth pass away, not one letter, not one stroke of a letter, will pass from the law until all is accomplished. Therefore, whoever breaks one of the least of these commandments, and teaches others to do the same, will be called least in the kingdom of heaven; but whoever does them and teaches them will be called great in the kingdom of heaven."

- What role do the law and the prophets play in the new covenant instituted by Jesus? This issue was critical for Jewish converts in the early church, as Matthew realized. It is still relevant for us today. Jesus speaks of fulfilling rather than abolishing the law and the prophets. What does that mean exactly?

- God of both law and grace, sometimes I'd like to think that spiritual laws and rules don't really apply to me. After all, we are saved through faith, not our good works. Yet the laws and instructions in both Old and New Testaments had purpose, and they were important to Jesus. Show me how to understand them in my life.

Thursday 8th March
Luke 11:14–23

Now he was casting out a demon that was mute; when the demon had gone out, the one who had been mute spoke, and the crowds were amazed. But some of them said, "He casts out demons by Beelzebul, the ruler of the demons." Others, to test him, kept demanding from him a sign from heaven. But he knew what they were thinking and said to them, "Every kingdom divided against itself becomes a desert, and house falls on house. If Satan also is divided against himself, how will his kingdom stand?—for you say that I cast out the demons by Beelzebul. Now if I cast out the demons by Beelzebul, by whom do your exorcists cast them out? Therefore they will be your judges. But if it is by the finger of God that I cast out the demons, then the kingdom of God has come to you.

When a strong man, fully armed, guards his castle, his property is safe. But when one stronger than he attacks him and overpowers him, he takes away his armor in which he trusted and divides his plunder. Whoever is not with me is against me, and whoever does not gather with me scatters."

- The core issue here is the source of Jesus' power when he expels demons from people. Is he tapping into the power of Beelzebul, the ruler of the demons, or is he calling on the power of God? If you were present, what would you have thought?

- Notice how Jesus points to his exorcisms (carried out with the power of God) as signs that the kingdom of God has come among us. This is true of all his miracles. Am I open to miracles in my life here and now? Do I truly want God's power to be evident?

Friday 9th March
Mark 12:28–34

One of the scribes came near and heard them disputing with one another, and seeing that Jesus answered them well, he asked him, "Which commandment is the first of all?" Jesus answered, "The first is, 'Hear, O Israel: the Lord our God, the Lord is one; you shall love the Lord your God with all your heart, and with all your soul, and with all your mind, and with all your strength.' The second is this, 'You shall love your neighbor as yourself.' There is no other commandment greater than these." Then the scribe said to him, "You are right, Teacher; you have truly said that 'he is one, and besides him there is no other'; and 'to love him with all the heart, and with all the understanding, and with all the strength,' and 'to love one's neighbor as oneself,'—this is much more important than all whole burnt offerings and sacrifices." When Jesus saw that he answered wisely, he said to him, "You are not far from the kingdom of God." After that no one dared to ask him any question.

• Loving God with our whole being, and loving our neighbor as we love ourselves—these two commitments, taken together, have greater priority than any and all other offerings. Love has priority over all other virtues.

• Are you comfortable with the designation of love as a *commandment*? The word can sound cold and legalistic whereas the word *love* evokes warmth and freedom. Could you suggest an alternative to "commandment"? Or would you want to?

Saturday 10th March
Luke 18:9–14

Jesus also told this parable to some who trusted in themselves that they were righteous and regarded others with contempt: "Two men went up to the temple to pray, one a Pharisee and the other a tax collector. The Pharisee, standing by himself, was praying thus, 'God, I thank you that I am not like other people: thieves, rogues, adulterers, or even like this tax collector. I fast twice a week; I give a tenth of all my income.' But the tax collector, standing far off, would not even look up to heaven, but was beating his breast and saying, 'God, be merciful to me, a sinner!' I tell you, this man went down to his home justified rather than the other; for all who exalt themselves will be humbled, but all who humble themselves will be exalted."

- This is a beautifully crafted parable whose meaning leaps off the page for us. Yet there is always more to learn from praying on it and asking Jesus to reveal its hidden depths. There may be some detail we had not noticed before or we may see how it applies to ourselves in a new light.

- It can be helpful to use our imagination and "become" one or the other of the characters. Notice how comfortable or uncomfortable we feel in his clothes. Try saying the prayer of each in turn. What is that like for you? Experience tells us that no one is wholly "Pharisee" (hypocrite) or wholly "tax collector" (truthfully self-aware).

March 11—March 17

Something to think and pray about each day this week:

Building the Kingdom

The Beatitudes are an insider's guide to the Christian life, inasmuch as they describe what it's like to be on mission in the world. Every customary marker of success, Jesus suggests, is wrong—and what appears to be difficult may in fact be a sign of fidelity to building God's kingdom.

I imagine what it might be like to be part of a great team embarking on a hoped-for championship season. The coach tells the team members of the hardships they will face, the struggles they will have to overcome in order to achieve victory. A good coach will be honest about what the team members must face so that they will not lose heart when, inevitably, things don't always go as hoped.

In the Beatitudes, Christ takes a similar approach, suggesting that the distant hope for building the kingdom will involve highs and lows. He tells his students that this mission will be arduous but that the reward will be heaven itself.

You'll know that you're building God's kingdom, Jesus says, when people "hate you, and when they exclude you, revile you, and defame you" (Luke 6:22), just as people did to the prophets. People hate those sent by God because such people always sting the consciences of the self-righteous. Jesus upset things through his outreach to lepers, to women, and to tax collectors and sinners. Today, Christians sting consciences through outreach to the poor, children yet to be born, immigrants and refugees, families, the sick, and many others.

Whose good is Christ calling you to serve? Are you willing to be reviled for the work to which Christ has called you? Are you willing to take a stand on behalf of those who have not the power to stand for themselves, and work tirelessly in the face of harassment? If so, Jesus says, you are blessed.

—Tim Muldoon, *The Ignatian Workout for Lent*

The Presence of God
I pause for a moment and think of the love and the grace that God showers on me. I am created in the image and likeness of God; I am God's dwelling place.

Freedom
Lord, you granted me the great gift of freedom. In these times, O Lord, grant that I may be free from any form of racism or intolerance. Remind me that we are all equal in your loving eyes.

Consciousness
Knowing that God loves me unconditionally, I can afford to be honest about how I am.
How has the day been, and how do I feel now? I share my feelings openly with the Lord.

The Word
I take my time to read the word of God slowly, a few times, allowing myself to dwell on anything that strikes me. (Please turn to the Scripture on the following pages. Inspiration points are there should you need them. When you are ready, return here to continue.)

Conversation

Sometimes I wonder what I might say if I were to meet you in person, Lord.
I think I might say "Thank you" because you are always there for me.

Conclusion

I thank God for these moments we have spent together and for any insights I have been given concerning the text.

Sunday 11th March
Fourth Sunday of Lent

John 3:14–21

Jesus said, "And just as Moses lifted up the serpent in the wilderness, so must the Son of Man be lifted up, that whoever believes in him may have eternal life. For God so loved the world that he gave his only Son, so that everyone who believes in him may not perish but may have eternal life. Indeed, God did not send the Son into the world to condemn the world, but in order that the world might be saved through him. Those who believe in him are not condemned; but those who do not believe are condemned already, because they have not believed in the name of the only Son of God. And this is the judgment, that the light has come into the world, and people loved darkness rather than light because their deeds were evil. For all who do evil hate the light and do not come to the light, so that their deeds may not be exposed. But those who do what is true come to the light, so that it may be clearly seen that their deeds have been done in God."

• God loved the world. This is my faith, Lord. Sometimes it seems to go against the evidence, when floods, earthquakes, droughts, and tsunamis devastate poor people. Central to my faith is the figure of Jesus, lifted on the Cross, knowing what it was to be devastated and a "failure," yet offering himself in love for us.

• God of all light, you continue to send light into the world and into my life. May I recognize it, thank you for it, and participate in its work.

Monday 12th March

John 4:43–54

When the two days were over, he went from that place to Galilee (for Jesus himself had testified that a prophet has no honor in the prophet's own country). When he came to Galilee, the Galileans welcomed him, since they had seen all that he had done in Jerusalem at the festival; for they too had gone to the festival. Then he came again to Cana in Galilee where he had changed the water into wine. Now there was a royal official whose son lay ill in Capernaum. When he heard that Jesus had come from Judea to Galilee, he went and begged him to come down and heal his son, for he was at the point of death. Then Jesus said to him, "Unless you see signs and wonders you will not believe." The official said to him, "Sir, come down before my little boy dies." Jesus said to him, "Go; your son will live." The man believed the word that Jesus spoke to him and started on his way. As he was going down, his slaves met him and told him that his child was alive. So he asked them the hour when he began to recover, and they said to him, "Yesterday at one in the afternoon the fever left him." The father realized that this was the hour when Jesus had said to him, "Your son will live." So he himself believed, along with his whole household. Now this was the second sign that Jesus did after coming from Judea to Galilee.

- John structures his presentation of the public life of Jesus around seven "signs." The first is the turning of water into wine at Cana (Jn. 2:1–11). Today's reading describes the second. For John, a sign is not just an unusual external event but a mysterious happening that reveals God and leads to faith. The royal official, desperately trying to save his dying son, begs Jesus to heal him. When Jesus assures him that his son will live, "The man believed the word that Jesus spoke to him."

- This story also illustrates how Jesus does not discriminate when someone is in need. In the previous chapter, he reaches out to the Samaritan woman. Here he helps a Gentile. He has come as Savior of the world. In my personal world today, who might need to encounter Jesus?

Tuesday 13th March
John 5:1–16

After this there was a festival of the Jews, and Jesus went up to Jerusalem. Now in Jerusalem by the Sheep Gate there is a pool, called in Hebrew Beth-zatha, which has five porticoes. In these lay many invalids—blind, lame, and paralyzed. One man was there who had been ill for thirty-eight years. When Jesus saw him lying there and knew that he had been there a long time, he said to him, "Do you want to be made well?" The sick man answered him, "Sir, I have no one to put me into the pool when the water is stirred up; and while I am making my way, someone else steps down ahead of me." Jesus said to him, "Stand up, take your mat and walk." At once the man was made well, and he took up his mat and began to walk. // Now that day was a sabbath. So the Jews said to the man who had been cured, "It is the sabbath; it is not lawful for you to carry your mat." But he answered them, "The man who made me well said to me, 'Take up your mat and walk.'" They asked him, "Who is the man who said to you, 'Take it up and walk'?" Now the man who had been healed did not know who it was, for Jesus had disappeared in the crowd that was there. Later Jesus found him in the temple and said to him, "See, you have been made well! Do not sin any more, so that nothing worse happens to you." The man went away and told the Jews that it was Jesus who had made him well. Therefore the Jews started persecuting Jesus, because he was doing such things on the sabbath.

- The anonymous man lying by the pool called Beth-zatha had waited thirty-eight years for healing. He might be described as "living with desire" all that time. Our prayers are not always answered immediately. We have to "live with desire." Remember T. S. Eliot's line: "But the faith and the love and the hope are all in the waiting."

- The opponents of Jesus criticize the man who had been cured—for carrying his mat on the Sabbath. We think of kindness as attractive; yet here a compassionate act by Jesus evokes hostility. Have you ever seen a person's goodness evoking an evil response?

Wednesday 14th March
John 5:17–30

But Jesus answered them, "My Father is still working, and I also am working." For this reason the Jews were seeking all the more to kill him, because he was not only breaking the sabbath, but was also calling God his own Father, thereby making himself equal to God. // Jesus said to them, "Very truly, I tell you, the Son can do nothing on his own, but only what he sees the Father doing; for whatever the Father does, the Son does likewise. The Father loves the Son and shows him all that he himself is doing; and he will show him greater works than these, so that you will be astonished. Indeed, just as the Father raises the dead and gives them life, so also the Son gives life to whomsoever he wishes. The Father judges no one but has given all judgment to the Son, so that all may honor the Son just as they honor the Father. Anyone who does not honor the Son does not honor the Father who sent him. Very truly, I tell you, anyone who hears my word and believes him who sent me has eternal life, and does not come under judgment, but has passed from death to life. Very truly, I tell you, the hour is coming, and is now here, when the dead will hear the voice of the Son of God, and those who hear will live. For just as the Father has life in himself, so he has granted the Son also to have life in himself; and he has given him authority to execute judgment, because he is the Son of Man. Do not be astonished at this; for the hour is coming when all who are in their graves will hear his voice and will come out—those who have done good, to the resurrection of life, and those who have done evil, to the resurrection of condemnation. I can do nothing on my own. As I hear, I judge; and my judgment is just, because I seek to do not my own will but the will of him who sent me."

- The relationship between Jesus and his heavenly Father is the topic in this enigmatic passage. Jesus traces everything in his being and in his choices to their source in the Father. "I can do nothing on my own." He and his Father are intertwined in every way, so much so that they are one (Jn. 10:30).

- Note the striking statement: "My Father is still working, and I also am working." God is present among us, but this is not a passive presence. It is an active presence through which God is involved in the drama of our lives as a fellow actor or partner.

Thursday 15th March
John 5:31–47

Jesus said, "If I testify about myself, my testimony is not true. There is another who testifies on my behalf, and I know that his testimony to me is true. You sent messengers to John, and he testified to the truth. Not that I accept such human testimony, but I say these things so that you may be saved. He was a burning and shining lamp, and you were willing to rejoice for a while in his light. But I have a testimony greater than John's. The works that the Father has given me to complete, the very works that I am doing, testify on my behalf that the Father has sent me. And the Father who sent me has himself testified on my behalf. You have never heard his voice or seen his form, and you do not have his word abiding in you, because you do not believe him whom he has sent. You search the scriptures because you think that in them you have eternal life; and it is they that testify on my behalf. Yet you refuse to come to me to have life. I do not accept glory from human beings. But I know that you do not have the love of God in you. I have come in my Father's name, and you do not accept me; if another comes in his own name, you will accept him. How can you believe when you accept glory from one another and do not seek the glory that comes from the one who alone is God? Do not think that I will accuse you before the Father; your accuser is Moses, on whom you have set your hope. If you believed Moses, you would believe me, for he wrote about me. But if you do not believe what he wrote, how will you believe what I say?"

- Who is Jesus? This is the core question being teased out in today's reading. The answer hinges on his relationship to God (whom he calls his Father). A secondary question is: Who (or what) bears testimony (witness) to Jesus? John indicates four witnesses: John the Baptist, the works of Jesus himself, the Father, and the Scriptures. Do you understand this style of argument?

- Who is Jesus? John approaches the question from a Jewish religious and cultural perspective. How would you answer the question today from within your own cultural terms of reference? How would you answer it out of your personal experience of knowing him?

Friday 16th March
John 7:1–2, 10, 25–30

After this Jesus went about in Galilee. He did not wish to go about in Judea because the Jews were looking for an opportunity to kill him. Now the Jewish festival of Booths was near. // But after his brothers had gone to the festival, then he also went, not publicly but as it were in secret. Now some of the people of Jerusalem were saying, "Is not this the man whom they are trying to kill? And here he is, speaking openly, but they say nothing to him! Can it be that the authorities really know that this is the Messiah? Yet we know where this man is from; but when the Messiah comes, no one will know where he is from." Then Jesus cried out as he was teaching in the temple, "You know me, and you know where I am from. I have not come on my own. But the one who sent me is true, and you do not know him. I know him, because I am from him, and he sent me." Then they tried to arrest him, but no one laid hands on him, because his hour had not yet come.

- The festival of Booths (or Tabernacles) commemorates the wandering of the Hebrew people in the desert, part of the first Exodus. Jesus' death and resurrection will constitute the second exodus.

- Jesus is claiming to be "from God" because he is sent. Note the number of times in John's Gospel that Jesus refers to God (or more usually his Father) as "the one who sent me." Is it possible to say that you and I are also sent because God is our Father too?

Saturday 17th March
John 7:40–53

When they heard these words, some in the crowd said, "This is really the prophet." Others said, "This is the Messiah." But some asked, "Surely the Messiah does not come from Galilee, does he? Has not the scripture said that the Messiah is descended from David and comes from Bethlehem, the village where David lived?" So there was a division in the crowd because of him. Some of them wanted to arrest him, but no one laid hands on him. // Then the temple police went back to the chief priests and Pharisees, who asked them, "Why did you not arrest him?" The police answered, "Never has anyone spoken like this!" Then the Pharisees replied, "Surely you have not been deceived too, have you? Has any one of the authorities or of the

Pharisees believed in him? But this crowd, which does not know the law—they are accursed." Nicodemus, who had gone to Jesus before, and who was one of them, asked, "Our law does not judge people without first giving them a hearing to find out what they are doing, does it?" They replied, "Surely you are not also from Galilee, are you? Search and you will see that no prophet is to arise from Galilee." Then each of them went home.

- The Jewish religious leaders and experts in the Law cannot agree on who Jesus is. Notice the constant appeal to the Old Testament. We may be more convinced by what the temple police report: "Never has anyone spoken like this!" Jesus speaks with integrity, wisdom, and authority. This impresses these unsophisticated men. They recognize the goodness of Jesus, which is hidden from the religious leaders.

- Pope Francis teaches that we must listen to the poor and the marginalized because they have a special insight into the reality of the world and of God. Who, in my daily encounters, might have authentic insight into the reality of God?

March 18—March 24

Something to think and pray about each day this week:

Keeping Hope

Viktor Frankl, the famous psychiatrist and concentration-camp survivor, observed in his important book *Man's Search for Meaning* that only those who had a reason to persevere in the horrific experience of the camps survived; those who lost hope quickly died. Quoting Nietzsche, he believed that "those who have a 'why' to live, can bear with almost any 'how.'" For Frankl, sacrifice is tolerable when it is meaningful.

The Evangelists portray Jesus as facing his suffering with resolve, not ignoring its reality, but choosing to enter it with his "face like flint." All four use the language of Psalm 22, described as "a poem of the person abandoned by God" or "a prayer of an innocent person." They also borrow the language and themes of the suffering servant of God, found in Isaiah, including the text above. They describe Jesus as fulfilling what Isaiah had described as a person who, in the midst of the great exile of Israel in Babylon, was called "to raise up the tribes of Jacob and to restore the survivors of Israel" (Isaiah 49:6) in order that God's salvation might reach to the ends of the earth. Jesus is faithful to his death.

Recalling the way Jesus approached his death, Paul would later write of how he himself thought nothing of the sufferings he faced.

> For I am convinced that neither death, nor life, nor angels, nor rulers, nor things present, nor things to come, nor powers, nor height, nor depth, nor anything else in all creation, will be able to separate us from the love of God in Christ Jesus our Lord.

—Romans 8:38–39

Following Jesus, and following Paul's understanding of what Jesus' sacrifice meant, our prayer is that we might live in fidelity to our God who loves us, with perfect readiness to go where he calls us, unafraid of the consequences of that call.

—Tim Muldoon, *The Ignatian Workout for Lent*

The Presence of God

Dear Jesus, today I call on you, but not to ask for anything. I'd like only to dwell in your presence. May my heart respond to your love.

Freedom

God my creator, you gave me life and the gift of freedom. Through your love I exist in this world. May I never take the gift of life for granted. May I always respect others' right to life.

Consciousness

I ask how I am today. Am I particularly tired, stressed, or anxious? If any of these characteristics apply, can I try to let go of the concerns that disturb me?

The Word

The word of God comes down to us through the Scriptures. May the Holy Spirit enlighten my mind and my heart to respond to the Gospel teachings. (Please turn to the Scripture on the following pages. Inspiration points are there should you need them. When you are ready, return here to continue.)

Conversation

I begin to talk with Jesus about the Scripture I have just read. What part of it strikes a chord in me? Perhaps the words of a friend—or some story I have heard recently—will rise to the surface in my consciousness. If so, does the story throw light on what the Scripture passage may be saying to me?

Conclusion

Glory be to the Father, and to the Son, and to the Holy Spirit,
As it was in the beginning, is now and ever shall be,
World without end. Amen.

Sunday 18th March
Fifth Sunday of Lent
John 12:20–33

Now among those who went up to worship at the festival were some Greeks. They came to Philip, who was from Bethsaida in Galilee, and said to him, "Sir, we wish to see Jesus." Philip went and told Andrew; then Andrew and Philip went and told Jesus. Jesus answered them, "The hour has come for the Son of Man to be glorified. Very truly, I tell you, unless a grain of wheat falls into the earth and dies, it remains just a single grain; but if it dies, it bears much fruit. Those who love their life lose it, and those who hate their life in this world will keep it for eternal life. Whoever serves me must follow me, and where I am, there will my servant be also. Whoever serves me, the Father will honor. // Now my soul is troubled. And what should I say—'Father, save me from this hour'? No, it is for this reason that I have come to this hour. Father, glorify your name." Then a voice came from heaven, "I have glorified it, and I will glorify it again." The crowd standing there heard it and said that it was thunder. Others said, "An angel has spoken to him." Jesus answered, "This voice has come for your sake, not for mine. Now is the judgment of this world; now the ruler of this world will be driven out. And I, when I am lifted up from the earth, will draw all people to myself." He said this to indicate the kind of death he was to die.

- The humble wish of the Greeks is to see Jesus. Lord, that is my wish also. That is why I give this time to prayer. May I see you more clearly, love you more dearly, and follow you more nearly, as the ancient prayer puts it.

- Jesus, in this time of prayer I imagine you putting a grain of wheat into my hand. You and I talk about what it can mean. When I next eat bread, it will have a deeper significance for me. When I share in the Eucharist, I will try to be aware that it means your own life, which is blessed, broken, shared, and consumed for the life of the world.

Monday 19th March
Saint Joseph, Spouse of the Blessed Virgin Mary
Matthew 1:16, 18–21, 24

. . . and Jacob the father of Joseph the husband of Mary, of whom Jesus was born, who is called the Messiah. Now the birth of Jesus the Messiah took place in this way. When his mother Mary had been engaged to Joseph, but before they lived together, she was found to be with child from the Holy Spirit. Her husband Joseph, being a righteous man and unwilling to expose her to public disgrace, planned to dismiss her quietly. But just when he had resolved to do this, an angel of the Lord appeared to him in a dream and said, "Joseph, son of David, do not be afraid to take Mary as your wife, for the child conceived in her is from the Holy Spirit. She will bear a son, and you are to name him Jesus, for he will save his people from their sins." When Joseph awoke from sleep, he did as the angel of the Lord commanded him; he took her as his wife.

- Matthew invites us to ponder the birth of Jesus from the perspective of Joseph, betrothed to Mary. He finds himself in a moral dilemma when he learns of Mary's pregnancy, which has come about "before they lived together." He is a righteous man who wants to do what is best for everyone and what is in harmony with the will of God. An angel is sent to enlighten him.

- Not all the decisions we are faced with in life are clearly between right and wrong. We may have to operate in morally gray areas, or in so-called "no-win" situations (where we will be misunderstood no matter what choice we make). We need to tap into the experience of others and pray for the wisdom of God's Holy Spirit.

Tuesday 20th March

John 8:21–30

Again he said to them, "I am going away, and you will search for me, but you will die in your sin. Where I am going, you cannot come." Then the Jews said, "Is he going to kill himself? Is that what he means by saying, 'Where I am going, you cannot come'?" He said to them, "You are from below, I am from above; you are of this world, I am not of this world. I told you that you would die in your sins, for you will die in your sins unless you believe that I am he." They said to him, "Who are you?" Jesus said to them, "Why do I speak to you at all? I have much to say about you and much to condemn; but the one who sent me is true, and I declare to the world what I have heard from him." They did not understand that he was speaking to them about the Father. So Jesus said, "When you have lifted up the Son of Man, then you will realize that I am he, and that I do nothing on my own, but I speak these things as the Father instructed me. And the one who sent me is with me; he has not left me alone, for I always do what is pleasing to him." As he was saying these things, many believed in him.

- The discussion is quite heated. "You will die in your sins unless you believe that I am he." And further down: "When you have lifted up the Son of Man, then you will realize that I am he." Jesus hanging on the cross is the ultimate answer to the question "Who are you?"

- The readings of these days may need to be simplified when brought to prayer. You might take a single verse, or even a single phrase—for example, "The one who sent me is with me; he has not left me alone." Or sit quietly with the overall mystery of who Jesus is!

Wednesday 21st March
John 8:31–42

Then Jesus said to the Jews who had believed in him, "If you continue in my word, you are truly my disciples; and you will know the truth, and the truth will make you free." They answered him, "We are descendants of Abraham and have never been slaves to anyone. What do you mean by saying, 'You will be made free'?" // Jesus answered them, "Very truly, I tell you, everyone who commits sin is a slave to sin. The slave does not have a permanent place in the household; the Son has a place there forever. So if the Son makes you free, you will be free indeed. I know that you are descendants of Abraham; yet you look for an opportunity to kill me, because there is no place in you for my word. I declare what I have seen in the Father's presence; as for you, you should do what you have heard from the Father." // They answered him, "Abraham is our father." Jesus said to them, "If you were Abraham's children, you would be doing what Abraham did, but now you are trying to kill me, a man who has told you the truth that I heard from God. This is not what Abraham did. You are indeed doing what your father does." They said to him, "We are not illegitimate children; we have one father, God himself." Jesus said to them, "If God were your Father, you would love me, for I came from God and now I am here. I did not come on my own, but he sent me."

- "The truth will make you free." This is one of the most frequently quoted statements of Jesus. But what is the meaning of "truth" and what is the meaning of "free"? Jesus discusses these issues with his listeners. Such discussion continues to this day among believers and even unbelievers. But does the statement make sense to you experientially? Can you point to a situation in which being faced with the truth freed you from some unfreedom, addiction, obsession, or inner darkness?

- John will write much about love later in his Gospel and in his letters. But his use of the word in this reading comes as a surprise, as if it is out of place. Had you noticed?

Thursday 22nd March

John 8:51–59

"Very truly, I tell you, whoever keeps my word will never see death." The Jews said to him, "Now we know that you have a demon. Abraham died, and so did the prophets; yet you say, 'Whoever keeps my word will never taste death.' Are you greater than our father Abraham, who died? The prophets also died. Who do you claim to be?" Jesus answered, "If I glorify myself, my glory is nothing. It is my Father who glorifies me, he of whom you say, 'He is our God,' though you do not know him. But I know him; if I were to say that I do not know him, I would be a liar like you. But I do know him and I keep his word. Your ancestor Abraham rejoiced that he would see my day; he saw it and was glad." Then the Jews said to him, "You are not yet fifty years old, and have you seen Abraham?" Jesus said to them, "Very truly, I tell you, before Abraham was, I am." So they picked up stones to throw at him, but Jesus hid himself and went out of the temple.

- "Who do you claim to be?" The discussion about the identity of Jesus continues. This relentless questioning shows how important the issue is— then and now. But instead of leading to a meeting of minds, Jesus' arguments provoke his enemies even further. "They picked up stones to throw at him." His life is now in danger. Can you understand this hostility to Jesus?

- Note yet another "I am" statement: "Before Abraham was, I am." Jesus claims both preexistence and oneness with God.

Friday 23rd March
John 10:31–42

The Jews took up stones again to stone him. Jesus replied, "I have shown you many good works from the Father. For which of these are you going to stone me?" The Jews answered, "It is not for a good work that we are going to stone you, but for blasphemy, because you, though only a human being, are making yourself God." Jesus answered, "Is it not written in your law, 'I said, you are gods'? If those to whom the word of God came were called 'gods'—and the scripture cannot be annulled—can you say that the one whom the Father has sanctified and sent into the world is blaspheming because I said, 'I am God's Son'? If I am not doing the works of my Father, then do not believe me. But if I do them, even though you do not believe me, believe the works, so that you may know and understand that the Father is in me and I am in the Father." Then they tried to arrest him again, but he escaped from their hands. // He went away again across the Jordan to the place where John had been baptizing earlier, and he remained there. Many came to him, and they were saying, "John performed no sign, but everything that John said about this man was true." And many believed in him there.

- Another threat to stone Jesus is followed by another attempt to arrest him. In between, the debate rages on with the word "blasphemy" coming to the fore. Jesus is guilty of blasphemy (his opponents say), because "You, though only a human being, are making yourself God." This, of course, is the heart of the matter. Christian faith affirms that Jesus is fully human and fully divine.

- Jesus tries to get his listeners to pay attention to his works as well as to his words. His works also speak, communicate, witness, teach, reveal. Jesus can do these works only from the power and will of the Father. Can our own words and actions be traced so clearly back to the God who is our Father?

Saturday 24th March
John 11:45–56

Many of the Jews therefore, who had come with Mary and had seen what Jesus did, believed in him. But some of them went to the Pharisees and told them what he had done. So the chief priests and the Pharisees called a meeting of the council, and said, "What are we to do? This man is performing many signs. If we let him go on like this, everyone will believe in him, and the Romans will come and destroy both our holy place and our nation." But one of them, Caiaphas, who was high priest that year, said to them, "You know nothing at all! You do not understand that it is better for you to have one man die for the people than to have the whole nation destroyed." He did not say this on his own, but being high priest that year he prophesied that Jesus was about to die for the nation, and not for the nation only, but to gather into one the dispersed children of God. So from that day on they planned to put him to death. // Jesus therefore no longer walked about openly among the Jews, but went from there to a town called Ephraim in the region near the wilderness; and he remained there with the disciples. Now the Passover of the Jews was near, and many went up from the country to Jerusalem before the Passover to purify themselves. They were looking for Jesus and were asking one another as they stood in the temple, "What do you think? Surely he will not come to the festival, will he?"

- Caiaphas was a Sadducee—ruthless, political, determined to buttress the status quo and the privileges of his wealthy class. He used the argument of the powerful in every age: we must eliminate the awkward troublemaker in the name of the common good—meaning the comfort of those in power. But Caiaphas spoke more wisely than he knew. One man, Jesus, was to die for the people, and for you and me.

- Those appointed to be the community's spiritual leaders now plotted to kill Jesus. Is this shocking to you? Why, or why not? Have you known other leaders, spiritual or otherwise, who stooped to such evil?

March 25—March 31

Something to think and pray about each day this week:

That Little Lost Lamb

The Word of God pitched his tent among us, sinners who are in need of mercy. And we all must hasten to receive the grace he offers us. Instead, the Gospel of St. John continues, "his own people received him not" (1:11). We reject him too many times, we prefer to remain closed in our errors and the anxiety of our sins. But Jesus does not desist and never ceases to offer himself and his grace, which saves us! Jesus is patient; he knows how to wait, and he waits for us always. This is a message of hope, a message of salvation, ancient and ever new. And we are called to witness with joy to this message of the Gospel of life, to the Gospel of light, of hope, and of love. For Jesus' message is this: life, light, hope, and love.

Jesus is all mercy. Jesus is all love: he is God made man. Each one of us is that little lost lamb, the coin that was mislaid; each one of us is that son who has squandered his freedom on false idols, illusions of happiness, and has lost everything. But God does not forget us; the Father never abandons us. He is a patient father, always waiting for us! He respects our freedom, but he remains faithful forever. And when we come back to him, he welcomes us like children into his house, for he never ceases, not for one instant, to wait for us with love. And his heart rejoices over every child who returns. He is celebrating because he is joy. God has this joy, when one of us sinners goes to him and asks his forgiveness.

—Pope Francis, *The Joy of Discipleship*

The Presence of God

God is with me, but even more astounding, God is within me.

Let me dwell for a moment on God's life-giving presence
in my body, in my mind, in my heart,
as I sit here, right now.

Freedom

Lord, may I never take the gift of freedom for granted. You gave me the great blessing of freedom of spirit. Fill my spirit with your peace and joy.

Consciousness

I remind myself that I am in the presence of God, who is my strength in times of weakness and my comforter in times of sorrow.

The Word

I take my time to read the word of God slowly, a few times, allowing myself to dwell on anything that strikes me. (Please turn to the Scripture on the following pages. Inspiration points are there should you need them. When you are ready, return here to continue.)

Conversation

Jesus, you always welcomed little children when you walked on this earth. Teach me to have a childlike trust in you. Teach me to live in the knowledge that you will never abandon me.

Conclusion

Glory be to the Father, and to the Son, and to the Holy Spirit,
As it was in the beginning, is now and ever shall be,
World without end. Amen.

Sunday 25th March
Palm Sunday of the Passion of the Lord
Mark 15:16–39

Then the soldiers led him into the courtyard of the palace (that is, the governor's headquarters); and they called together the whole cohort. And they clothed him in a purple cloak; and after twisting some thorns into a crown, they put it on him. And they began saluting him, "Hail, King of the Jews!" They struck his head with a reed, spat upon him, and knelt down in homage to him. After mocking him, they stripped him of the purple cloak and put his own clothes on him. Then they led him out to crucify him. // They compelled a passer-by, who was coming in from the country, to carry his cross; it was Simon of Cyrene, the father of Alexander and Rufus. Then they brought Jesus to the place called Golgotha (which means the place of a skull). And they offered him wine mixed with myrrh; but he did not take it. And they crucified him, and divided his clothes among them, casting lots to decide what each should take. // It was nine o'clock in the morning when they crucified him. The inscription of the charge against him read, "The King of the Jews." And with him they crucified two bandits, one on his right and one on his left. Those who passed by derided him, shaking their heads and saying, "Aha! You who would destroy the temple and build it in three days, save yourself, and come down from the cross!" In the same way the chief priests, along with the scribes, were also mocking him among themselves and saying, "He saved others; he cannot save himself. Let the Messiah, the King of Israel, come down from the cross now, so that we may see and believe." Those who were crucified with him also taunted him. // When it was noon, darkness came over the whole land until three in the afternoon. At three o'clock Jesus cried out with a loud voice, "Eloi, Eloi, lema sabachthani?" which means, "My God, my God, why have you forsaken me?" When some of the bystanders heard it, they said, "Listen, he is calling for Elijah." And someone ran, filled a sponge with sour wine, put it on a stick, and gave it to him to drink, saying, "Wait, let us see whether Elijah will come to take him down." Then Jesus gave a loud cry and breathed his last. And the curtain of the temple was torn in two, from top to bottom. Now when the centurion, who stood facing him, saw that in this way he breathed his last, he said, "Truly this man was God's Son!"

- Where would I be in this drama? Which person in the crowd? What would I think of all I witnessed? How would my heart respond?

- Lord, help me walk with you on this dark journey. Teach me how to share in your pain but also in your faith.

Monday 26th March
Monday of Holy Week

John 12:1–11

Six days before the Passover Jesus came to Bethany, the home of Lazarus, whom he had raised from the dead. There they gave a dinner for him. Martha served, and Lazarus was one of those at the table with him. Mary took a pound of costly perfume made of pure nard, anointed Jesus' feet, and wiped them with her hair. The house was filled with the fragrance of the perfume. But Judas Iscariot, one of his disciples (the one who was about to betray him), said, 'Why was this perfume not sold for three hundred denarii and the money given to the poor?' (He said this not because he cared about the poor, but because he was a thief; he kept the common purse and used to steal what was put into it.) Jesus said, "Leave her alone. She bought it so that she might keep it for the day of my burial. You always have the poor with you, but you do not always have me." // When the great crowd of the Jews learned that he was there, they came not only because of Jesus but also to see Lazarus, whom he had raised from the dead. So the chief priests planned to put Lazarus to death as well, since it was on account of him that many of the Jews were deserting and were believing in Jesus.

- The home of Martha and Mary in Bethany was always a place of welcome and refuge for Jesus. With his life increasingly under threat he chooses to enjoy a meal there with his friends. But Mary's action of anointing his feet with costly perfume causes friction. Judas, who was also present, objects to such extravagance. Jesus defends Mary and links her action with his coming death and burial.

- Whose side are you on? Perhaps you can see some validity in what Judas says. Yet it is Mary who continues to be admired for her loving and uninhibited gesture.

Tuesday 27th March
Tuesday of Holy Week
John 13:21–33, 36–38

After saying this Jesus was troubled in spirit, and declared, "Very truly, I tell you, one of you will betray me." The disciples looked at one another, uncertain of whom he was speaking. One of his disciples—the one whom Jesus loved—was reclining next to him; Simon Peter therefore motioned to him to ask Jesus of whom he was speaking. So while reclining next to Jesus, he asked him, "Lord, who is it?" Jesus answered, "It is the one to whom I give this piece of bread when I have dipped it in the dish." So when he had dipped the piece of bread, he gave it to Judas

son of Simon Iscariot. After he received the piece of
bread, Satan entered into him. Jesus said to him, "Do
quickly what you are going to do." Now no one at the
table knew why he said this to him. Some thought
that, because Judas had the common purse, Jesus was
telling him, "Buy what we need for the festival"; or,
that he should give something to the poor. So, after receiving the piece of bread, he immediately went
out. And it was night. // When he had gone out, Jesus
said, "Now the Son of Man has been glorified, and
God has been glorified in him. If God has been glorified in him, God will also glorify him in himself and
will glorify him at once. Little children, I am with
you only a little longer. You will look for me; and as
I said to the Jews so now I say to you, 'Where I am
going, you cannot come.'" // Simon Peter said to him,
"Lord, where are you going?" Jesus answered, "Where
I am going, you cannot follow me now; but you will
follow afterwards." Peter said to him, "Lord, why can
I not follow you now? I will lay down my life for you."
Jesus answered, "Will you lay down your life for me?
Very truly, I tell you, before the cock crows, you will
have denied me three times."

- Imagine yourself reclining at the table during
  the Last Supper. Are you picking up the tensions
  among the other participants? Do you notice how
  Jesus is "troubled in spirit"? Have you sensed his

inner turmoil as one of his friends is plotting to betray him? Let the drama of the scene draw you into it. What are your predominant feelings? Speak freely to Jesus about the whole situation and your reactions to it.

- Toward the end of the reading we see Peter boasting and blustering and making a fool of himself. Jesus reads the human heart and knows Peter. Far from laying down his life for Jesus, Peter will soon be denying (three times!) that he ever knew him. What would you say to Peter if you were there?

Wednesday 28th March
Wednesday of Holy Week
Matthew 26:14–25

Then one of the twelve, who was called Judas Iscariot, went to the chief priests and said, "What will you give me if I betray him to you?" They paid him thirty pieces of silver. And from that moment he began to look for an opportunity to betray him. // On the first day of Unleavened Bread the disciples came to Jesus, saying, "Where do you want us to make the preparations for you to eat the Passover?" He said, "Go into the city to a certain man, and say to him, 'The Teacher says, My time is near; I will keep the Passover at your house with my disciples.'" So the disciples did as Jesus had directed them, and they prepared the Passover meal. // When it was evening, he took his place with the twelve; and while they were eating, he said, "Truly I tell you, one of you will betray me." And they became greatly distressed and began to say to him one after another, "Surely not I, Lord?" He answered, "The one who has dipped his hand into the bowl with me will betray me. The Son of Man goes as it is written of him, but woe to that one by whom the Son of Man is betrayed! It would have been better for that one not to have been born." Judas, who betrayed him, said, "Surely not I, Rabbi?" He replied, "You have said so."

- In some places this day is known as Spy Wednesday. Judas is the "spy" or sly, sneaky person who secretly approaches the chief priests with the intention of betraying Jesus to them. Like all such spies he is looking for a reward and agrees on thirty pieces of silver. The naming of the price is meant to shock us. Is this all that the life of the Son of Man is worth?

- Jesus uses only words to persuade Judas not to carry out his pact with the chief priests. He takes no other measures that might prevent his arrest. Does this surprise you? Can you understand it?

Thursday 29th March
Thursday of Holy Week (Holy Thursday)
John 13:1–15

Now before the festival of the Passover, Jesus knew that his hour had come to depart from this world and go to the Father. Having loved his own who were in the world, he loved them to the end. The devil had already put it into the heart of Judas son of Simon Iscariot to betray him. And during supper Jesus, knowing that the Father had given all things into his hands, and that he had come from God and was going to God, got up from the table, took off his outer robe, and tied a towel around himself. Then he poured water into a basin and began to wash the disciples' feet and to wipe them with the towel that was tied around him. He came to Simon Peter, who said to him, "Lord, are you going to wash my feet?" Jesus answered, "You do not know now what I am doing, but later you will understand." Peter said to him, "You will never wash my feet." Jesus answered, "Unless I wash you, you have no share with me." Simon Peter said to him, "Lord, not my feet only but also my hands and my head!" Jesus said to him, "One who has bathed does not need to wash, except for the feet, but is entirely clean. And you are clean, though not all of you." For he knew who was to betray him; for this reason he said, "Not all of you are clean." // After he had washed their feet, had put on his robe, and had returned to the table, he said to them, "Do you know what I have done to you? You call me Teacher and Lord—and you are right, for that is what I am. So if I, your Lord and Teacher, have washed your feet, you also ought to wash one another's feet. For I have set you an example, that you also should do as I have done to you."

- John introduces this story with great solemnity. He takes care to specify precisely the point in Jesus' life when he decides to wash his disciples' feet. Afterwards, Jesus explains the meaning of what he has done. He holds it up as an example for the apostles to follow. They are to express love within their community with humility and in practical ways. Note that this service is to be mutual: "to wash one another's feet." What are you called to do in your life circumstances?

- There is no description of the institution of the Eucharist in John's Gospel. Commentators see the washing of the feet as taking its place. Do you grasp the common values that underlie both events?

Friday 30th March
Friday of the Passion of the Lord
(Good Friday)

John 18:1—19:42

After Jesus had spoken these words, he went out with his disciples across the Kidron valley to a place where there was a garden, which he and his disciples entered. Now Judas, who betrayed him, also knew the place, because Jesus often met there with his disciples. So Judas brought a detachment of soldiers together with police from the chief priests and the Pharisees, and they came there with lanterns and torches and weapons. Then Jesus, knowing all that was to happen to him, came forward and asked them, "Whom are you looking for?" They answered, "Jesus of Nazareth." Jesus replied, "I am he." Judas, who betrayed him, was standing with them. When Jesus said to them, "I am he," they stepped back and fell to the ground. Again he asked them, "Whom are you looking for?" And they said, "Jesus of Nazareth." Jesus answered, "I told you that I am he. So if you are looking for me, let these men go." This was to fulfill the word that he had spoken, "I did not lose a single one of those whom you gave me." Then Simon Peter, who had a sword, drew it, struck the high priest's slave, and cut off his right ear. The slave's name was Malchus. Jesus said to Peter, "Put your sword back into its sheath. Am I not to drink the cup that the Father has given me?" // So the soldiers, their officer, and the Jewish police arrested Jesus and bound him. First they took him to Annas, who was the father-in-law of Caiaphas, the high priest that year. Caiaphas was the one who had advised the Jews that it was better to have one person die for the people. . . . // Then the high priest questioned Jesus about his disciples and about his teaching. Jesus answered, "I have spoken openly to the world; I have always taught in synagogues and in the temple, where all the Jews come together. I have said nothing in secret. Why do you ask me? Ask those who heard what I said to them; they know what I said." When he had said this, one of the police standing nearby struck Jesus on the face, saying, "Is that how you answer the high priest?" Jesus answered, "If I have spoken wrongly, testify to the wrong. But if I have spoken rightly, why do you strike me?" Then Annas sent him bound to Caiaphas the high priest. . . . // Then they took Jesus from Caiaphas to Pilate's headquarters. It was early in the morning. They themselves did not enter the headquarters, so as to avoid ritual defilement and to be able to eat the Passover. So Pilate went out to them and said, "What accusation do you bring against this man?" They answered, "If this man were not a criminal, we would not have handed him over to you." Pilate said to them, "Take him yourselves and judge him according to your law." The Jews replied, "We are not permitted to put anyone to death." (This was to fulfill what Jesus had said when he indicated the kind of death he was to die.) // Then Pilate entered the headquarters again, summoned Jesus, and asked him, "Are you the King of the Jews?" Jesus answered, "Do you ask this on your own, or did others tell you about me?" Pilate replied, "I am not a Jew, am I? Your own nation and the chief priests have handed you over to me. What have you done?" Jesus answered, "My kingdom is not from this world. If my kingdom were from this world, my followers would be fighting to keep me from being handed over to the Jews. But as it is, my kingdom is not from here." Pilate asked him, "So you are a king?" Jesus answered, "You say that I am a king. For this I was born, and for this I came into the world, to testify to the truth. Everyone who belongs to the truth listens to my voice." Pilate asked him, "What is truth?" // After he had said this, he went out to the Jews again and told them, "I find no case against him. But you have a custom that I release someone for you at the Passover. Do you want me to release for you the King of the Jews?" They shouted in reply, "Not this man, but Barabbas!" Now Barabbas was a bandit. . . . // [Pilate] asked Jesus, "Where are you from?" But Jesus gave him no answer. Pilate therefore said to him, "Do you refuse to speak to me? Do you not know that I have power to release you, and power to crucify you?" Jesus answered him, "You would have no power over me unless it had been given you from above; therefore the one who handed me over to you is guilty of a greater sin." From then on Pilate tried to release him, but the Jews cried out, "If you release this man, you are no friend of the emperor. Everyone who claims to be a king sets himself against the emperor." // When Pilate heard these words, he brought Jesus outside and sat on the judge's bench at a place called The Stone Pavement, or in Hebrew Gabbatha. Now it was the day of Preparation for the Passover; and it was about noon. He said to the Jews, "Here is your King!" They cried out, "Away with him! Away with him! Crucify him!" Pilate asked them, "Shall I crucify your King?" The chief priests answered, "We have no king but the emperor." Then he handed him over to them to be crucified. // So they took Jesus; and carrying the cross by himself, he went out to what is called The Place of the Skull, which in Hebrew is called Golgotha. There they crucified him, and with him two others, one on either side, with Jesus between them. Pilate also had an inscription written and put on the cross. It read, "Jesus of Nazareth, the King of the Jews." Many of the Jews read this inscription, because the place where Jesus was crucified was near the city; and it was written in Hebrew, in Latin, and in Greek. Then the chief priests of the Jews said to Pilate, "Do not write, 'The King of the Jews,' but, 'This man said, I am King of the Jews.'" Pilate answered, "What I have written I have written." When the soldiers had crucified Jesus, they took his clothes and divided them into four parts, one for each soldier. They also took his tunic; now the tunic was seamless, woven in one piece from the top. So they said to one another, "Let us not tear it, but cast lots for it to see who will get it." This was to fulfill what the scripture says,

"They divided my clothes among themselves,
    and for my clothing they cast lots."

And that is what the soldiers did.

Meanwhile, standing near the cross of Jesus were his mother, and his mother's sister, Mary the wife of Clopas, and Mary Magdalene. When Jesus saw his mother and the disciple whom he loved standing beside her, he said to his mother, "Woman, here is your son." Then he said to the disciple, "Here is your mother." And from that hour the disciple took her into his own home. // After this, when Jesus knew that all was now finished, he said (in order to fulfill the scripture), "I am thirsty." A jar full of sour wine was standing there. So they put a sponge full of the wine on a branch of hyssop and held it to his mouth. When Jesus had received the wine, he said, "It is finished." Then he bowed his head and gave up his spirit. . . . //

After these things, Joseph of Arimathea, who was a disciple of Jesus, though a secret one because of his fear of the Jews, asked Pilate to let him take away the body of Jesus. Pilate gave him permission; so he came and removed his body. Nicodemus, who had at first come to Jesus by night, also came, bringing a mixture of myrrh and aloes, weighing about a hundred pounds. They took the body of Jesus and wrapped it with the spices in linen cloths, according to the burial custom of the Jews. Now there was a garden in the place where he was crucified, and in the garden there was a new tomb in which no one had ever been laid. And so, because it was the Jewish day of Preparation, and the tomb was nearby, they laid Jesus there.

- Good Friday puts the cross before me and challenges me not to look away. If I have followed Jesus' footsteps to Calvary, I do not have to fear because I, like him, am confident in God's enduring presence.

- Wherever there is suffering or pain, I seek the face of Jesus. I ask him for the strength I need to be a sign of hope wherever there is despair, to be a presence of love wherever it is most needed.

Saturday 31st March
Holy Saturday

Mark 16:1–7

When the sabbath was over, Mary Magdalene, and Mary the mother of James, and Salome bought spices, so that they might go and anoint him. And very early on the first day of the week, when the sun had risen, they went to the tomb. They had been saying to one another, "Who will roll away the stone for us from the entrance to the tomb?" When they looked up, they saw that the stone, which was very large, had already been rolled back. As they entered the tomb, they saw a young man, dressed in a white robe, sitting on the right side; and they were alarmed. But he said to them, "Do not be alarmed; you are looking for Jesus of Nazareth, who was crucified. He has been raised; he is not here. Look, there is the place they laid him. But go, tell his disciples and Peter that he is going ahead of you to Galilee; there you will see him, just as he told you."

• Angels could have come to the women in their homes, couldn't they? But they allowed them to make the sorrowful walk to the tomb. They needed to see for themselves that it was empty. They had to experience the surprise, the shock, then the alarm when the angel appeared to them. God does not eliminate our need for learning and perceiving, step-by-step.

- No sooner have they understood that Jesus has been raised than they are given the crucial task of taking this news to the disciples. We see the love and bravery of these women, who did not run from the scene and panic but stood their ground and listened to God's message. Lord, may I develop this kind of sturdy faith in you.

Easter
April 1

Something to think and pray about today.

The Moments That Surprise

Vulnerability opens us to God's surprises. Mary Magdalene was surprised when Christ called her name. Peter and his fellow fishermen were surprised by the sudden pull in their casted nets. Thomas was surprised by the solidness of the person in front of him. The men walking the road to Emmaus were surprised by their guest at table, later noticing the longing within themselves: "Were not our hearts burning within us on the road?"

We too recognize the Resurrected Jesus in these moments of surprise—in a familiar voice calling us by name, in unexpected abundance, in a concrete experience of God's presence, in the breaking of the bread. These surprises are moments of recognition—when we know the Risen God is in our midst and that Easter is not a one-time event. The wait is over and daybreak comes. Joy surprises, and everywhere resurrection is happening.

—Elizabeth Eiland Figueroa on *dotMagis*,
the blog of *IgnatianSpirituality.com*
http://www.ignatianspirituality.com/21204/
waiting-for-daybreak

The Presence of God

Dear Lord, as I come to you today, fill my heart, my whole being, with the wonder of your presence. Help me remain receptive to you as I put aside the cares of this world. Fill my mind with your peace.

Freedom

Lord, grant me the grace to be free from the excesses of this life. Let me not get caught up with the desire for wealth. Keep my heart and mind free to love and serve you.

Consciousness

I exist in a web of relationships: links to nature, people, God.

I trace out these links, giving thanks for the life that flows through them.

Some links are twisted or broken; I may feel regret, anger, disappointment.

I pray for the gift of acceptance and forgiveness.

The Word

God speaks to each of us individually. I listen attentively, to hear what he is saying to me. Read the text a few times, then listen. (Please turn to the Scripture on the following pages. Inspiration points are there should you need them. When you are ready, return here to continue.)

Conversation

Jesus, you speak to me through the words of the Gospels. May I respond to your call today. Teach me to recognize your hand at work in my daily living.

Conclusion

I thank God for these moments we have spent together and for any insights I have been given concerning the text.

Sunday 1st April
Easter Sunday of the Resurrection of the Lord

Luke 24:13–35

Now on that same day two of them were going to a village called Emmaus, about seven miles from Jerusalem, and talking with each other about all these things that had happened. While they were talking and discussing, Jesus himself came near and went with them, but their eyes were kept from recognizing him. And he said to them, "What are you discussing with each other while you walk along?" They stood still, looking sad. Then one of them, whose name was Cleopas, answered him, "Are you the only stranger in Jerusalem who does not know the things that have taken place there in these days?" He asked them, "What things?" They replied, "The things about Jesus of Nazareth, who was a prophet mighty in deed and word before God and all the people, and how our chief priests and leaders handed him over to be condemned to death and crucified him. But we had hoped that he was the one to redeem Israel. Yes, and besides all this, it is now the third day since these things took place. Moreover, some women of our group astounded us. They were at the tomb early this morning, and when they did not find his body there, they came back and told us that they had indeed seen a vision of angels who said that he was alive. Some of those who were with us went to the tomb and found it just as the women had said; but they did not see him." Then he said to them, "Oh, how foolish you are, and how slow of heart to believe all that the prophets have declared! Was it not necessary that the Messiah should suffer these things and then enter into his glory?" Then beginning with Moses and all the prophets, he interpreted to them the things about himself in all the scriptures. // As they came near the village to which they were going, he walked ahead as if he were going on. But they urged him strongly, saying, "Stay with us, because it is almost evening and the day is now nearly over." So he went in to stay with them. When he was at the table with them, he took bread, blessed and broke it, and gave it to them. Then their eyes were opened, and they recognized him; and he vanished from their sight. They said to each other, "Were not our hearts burning within us while he was talking to us on the road, while he was opening the scriptures to us?" That same hour they got up and returned to Jerusalem; and they found the eleven and their companions gathered together. They were saying, "The Lord has risen indeed, and he has appeared to Simon!" Then they told what had happened on the road, and how he had been made known to them in the breaking of the bread.

- Sit at table with the disciples and Jesus in the inn at Emmaus. Notice the eucharistic overtones of what Jesus does with the bread. Each time we attend Mass, do we recognize him in the breaking of the bread?

- Are we like the two disciples in wanting to share their experience of the risen Lord? Even though it was night, they headed back to Jerusalem to share this news. Lord, I confess that I don't feel such urgency. But I am willing.